IN CHRIST

Who We Are and What We Have in Him : 40 Daily Bites

Bisi Oladipupo

Springs of life publishing

Copyright © 2024 by Bisi Oladipupo

Springs of life publishing

ISBN: (978-1-915269-44-7 (e-book)

ISBN: 978-1-915269-45-4 (paperback)

All Rights Reserved.

No part of this book may be used or reproduced by any means, graphic, electronic, or mechanical, including photocopying, recording, taping, or by any information storage retrieval system without the written permission of the publisher except in the case of brief quotations embodied in critical articles and reviews.

Printed in the United Kingdom

Unless otherwise indicated, scripture quotations are taken from the New King James Version.

Scripture taken from the New King James Version®. Copyright © 1982 by Thomas Nelson. Used by permission. All rights reserved.

Scripture quotations from The Authorized (King James) Version. Rights in the Authorized Version in the United Kingdom are vested in the Crown. Reproduced by permission of the Crown's patentee, Cambridge University Press.

Scripture quotations marked (AMP) are taken from the Amplified Bible, Copyright © 2015 by The Lockman Foundation. Used by permission.

Contents

	Dedication	VI
	Introduction	VII
1.	Day 1: Complete in Him	1
2.	Day 2: A New Creation in Christ	3
3.	Day 3: Partakers of His Promise in Christ	5
4.	Day 4: Our Life is Hid with Christ in God	7
5.	Day 5: Boldness and Access	9
6.	Day 6: Sit Together in Heavenly Places	11
7.	Day 7: Blessed with all Spiritual Blessings	13
8.	Day 8: Chosen in Him before the Foundation of the World	15
9.	Day 9: Accepted in the Beloved	17

10.	Day 10: Redemption Through His Blood	19
11.	Day 11: We Have Obtained an Inheritance	21
12.	Day 12: We are His Workmanship Created in Christ Jesus	23
13.	Day 13: Near to God by the Blood of Jesus	25
14.	Day 14: We Access to the Father	27
15.	Day 15: All the Promises of God are Yes in Christ	29
16.	Day 16: The Righteousness of God in Him	31
17.	Day 17: God Dwells in Us	33
18.	Day 18: We are in Christ	34
19.	Day 19: We Are Saved From Wrath Through Him	36
20.	Day 20: More Than Conquerors Through Him	38
21.	Day 21: Enriched By Him	40
22.	Day 22: We live through Him	42
23.	Day 23: Called unto the Fellowship of His Son	44
24.	Day 24: We are Now Light in the Lord	46
25.	Day 25: We Are Now Sons of God	48
26.	Day 26: Joint Heirs with Christ	50
27.	Day 27: Our Old Man Is Crucified with Him	52
28.	Day 28: We Are to Walk as He Walked	54
29.	Day 29: We Have Eternal Life	55

30.	Day 30: No Condemnation to Those in Christ Jesus	57
31.	Day 31: Greater Is He That Is in You	59
32.	Day 32: We Always Triumph in Christ	61
33.	Day 33: : In Christ, the Veil Is Taken Away From Our Hearts	63
34.	Day 34: We Are All One in Christ	65
35.	Day 35: Dead Unto Sin and Alive Unto God	67
36.	Day 36: God Loves Us as He Loves Jesus	69
37.	Day 37: We Have Put on Christ	71
38.	Day 38: We Have the Promise of the Holy Spirit	73
39.	Day 39: In Christ, Our Faith Works Through Love	75
40.	Day 40: In Him We Have Peace	77
Salvation Prayer		79
About the author		81
Also by		82

To Jesus Christ, my Lord and Saviour to Him alone that laid down His life so that I might have eternal life. To Him that led captivity captive and gave gifts unto men (Ephesians 4 8). One of those gifts is writing!

Bisi Oladipupo

Introduction

Why do we need to know who we are in Christ?

As believers in Christ, we have been translated into another kingdom. The kingdom of our Lord Jesus Christ (Colossians 1:13). 2 Corinthians 5:17 reads, *"Therefore, if anyone is in Christ, he is a new creation; old things have passed away; behold, all things have become new"*. Notice the word "in Christ". This is exactly our position when we give our lives to the Lord and make Him our Lord and Saviour. We are now in Christ—a new creation in Christ.

In the natural, if we place something in a thing, it would benefit from the environment in which it has been placed. A foetus in a mother's womb benefits from everything that the mother has to offer. Why? Because the foetus is in the mother's womb.

This kingdom that we have been translated into works by knowledge: *"And you shall know the truth, and the truth shall make you free"* (John 8:32). The Book of Isaiah also tells us that we are justified by the knowledge of Him (Isaiah 53:11). Knowledge of what? Knowledge of what the Lord has done for us. These are all spiritual realities that must be acknowledged in order for us to walk in the revelation of them. These things are real, and we cannot afford to walk in ignorance.

We are now in Christ and need to know who we are in Him. The enemy knows that we are now in Christ. Remember the seven sons of Sceva, a Jewish high priest in the Book of Acts who tried to cast out demons in the name of Jesus, whom Paul preached? This was the response of the evil spirit: *And the evil spirit answered and said, "Jesus I know, and Paul I know; but who are you?"* (Acts 19:15). Do you think he knew Paul after the flesh? No, but who Paul was in the spirit.

When we know who we are in Christ, it will give us boldness because this walk is not about us; it is all about "Christ in us" (Colossians 1:27) and we in Him (Acts 17:28).

The Scripture tells us to be strong in the Lord and in the power of His might (Ephesians 6:10). We are not told to be strong in ourselves but in Christ. The more we know what we have in Christ and wrapped up in Him, the more aware we will become, which will reflect in our Christian walk in this present world.

So, let us go on a forty-day journey to discover "Who we are in Christ". Meditate on the scriptures and go over them again and again. For indeed, we do need to know who we really are in Christ.

Bisi

Day 1: Complete in Him

"For in Him dwells all the fullness of the Godhead [f]bodily; 10 and you are complete in Him, who is the head of all [g]principality and power" (Colossians 2:9-10).

Sometimes, we find ourselves alone. You could be in a place where you cannot call on someone else in person. At those times, we must remember that we are complete in Him. Jesus Christ makes us complete; therefore, we are never alone. Jesus Christ makes us complete because all the fulness of the Godhead dwells in Him.

Remember that before the disciples left Jesus, just before He was going to be betrayed, Jesus told His disciples that they would abandon Him, but He was not alone because the Father was with Him (John 16:32).

When you are alone, remind yourself: *"I am complete in Him"*. You are never alone; you are complete in Him. Did someone leave you? Does someone no longer want you? Be reminded that I am complete in Him. Or you could find yourself on a project alone. Heaven is there with you. You are not alone.

"For it pleased the Father that in Him all the fullness should dwell" (Colossians 1:19).

"And of His fullness we have all received, and grace for grace" (John 1:16).

Another perspective of the scripture in Colossians 2 verse 10 is that we have access to everything Jesus has provided us. Our authority is because Jesus gave us authority (Matthew 28:18). We just have to grow in the knowledge of our authority because we are indeed complete in Him.

We have access to the Father because of Jesus (John 14:6) and the person of the Holy Spirit (John 14:16). We have access to the fullness of the Godhead because of Jesus Christ.

Prayer: Father, I thank You that I am complete in Christ. There is nothing missing or broken. I am fully complete in Him. I can walk with my head up because I am complete in Him.

Day 2: A New Creation in Christ

Therefore, if anyone is in Christ, he is a new creation; old things have passed away; behold, all things have become new; Now all things are of God, who has reconciled us to Himself through Jesus Christ, and has given us the ministry of reconciliation (2 Corinthians 5:17-18).

Any man in Christ is a new creation. New is exactly what it means. If anyone gave you something brand new, would you start looking for anything old in it? No, not at all, because there would be no need for that.

The same applies when our spirits become new in Christ Jesus. Our spirits now have life because of righteousness (Romans 8:10). We will begin to pick things up and have leadings in our spirits because we have now become alive unto God (Romans 6:14). Whether or not we obey and yield to those leadings is another topic. However, the fact is, as new creations in Christ Jesus, our spirits become alive unto God. What a privilege!

The preceding verse also tells us that we have been given a ministry of reconciliation. We are told to tell others about Jesus Christ. It is a ministry for everyone (not just a select few), for we who are now in Christ Jesus.

May we be sensitive to the fact that our spirits are now alive unto God.

Prayer: Father, I thank You that I am now in Christ Jesus. My spirit is now life because of righteousness, and I am alive unto God.

Day 3: Partakers of His Promise in Christ

"That the Gentiles should be fellow heirs, and of the same body, and partakers of his promise in Christ by the gospel" (Ephesians 3:6; KJV).

[it is this:] that the Gentiles are now joint heirs [with the Jews] and members of the same body, and joint partakers [sharing] in the [same divine] promise in Christ Jesus through [their faith in] the good news [of salvation] (Ephesians 3:6; AMP).

Now, in Christ, we are fellow heirs of the same body—the body of Christ and partakers of the promise in Christ. The good news is that the gospel has given us access to these amazing benefits in Christ.

According to the Book of Galatians, we are now the Israel of God (Galatians 6:16).

We need to meditate on this.

Prayer: Father, I thank You that I am now a fellow heir and partaker of the promises in Christ.

Day 4: Our Life is Hid with Christ in God

"*For you died, and your life is hidden with Christ in God*" (Colossians 3:3).

Only the Lord knows the purpose He has for us individually. Our life purpose is hidden with Christ in God.

Our role is to find out God's plans for our lives, which are already hidden in Christ. Nobody else knows your potential but the Lord and whosoever the Lord reveals it to. We must not allow circumstances or other voices to put limits on us. We have a great purpose in Christ.

This could be one reason others do not always see our potential. Only those with spiritual discernment can discern our potential because it is hidden. It will take spiritual discernment for others to see them and for us also to see the potential in others.

Another application of this scripture of *"our lives are hidden in Christ in God"* is divine protection. We are indeed hidden with Christ in God.

Prayer: Father, I thank You that my life is hidden with Christ in God. You care and love me so much that You found it fit to hide my life with Christ. Thank You, Father.

Day 5: Boldness and Access

In whom we have boldness and access with confidence by the faith of him (Ephesians 3:12; KJV).

What a great privilege we have in Christ! Because of Jesus Christ, we can now come boldly unto God. We can come boldly unto the throne of grace (Hebrews 4:16). We now have access with confidence, knowing that God will answer our prayers in line with His will.

This is the confidence that we now have in Him.

"And this is the confidence that we have in him, that, if we ask any thing according to his will, he heareth us" (1 John 5:14; KJV).

Prayer: Father, I thank You that because of Jesus, I can now come boldly to You. I thank You because I now have confidence that You hear my prayers.

DAY 6: SIT TOGETHER IN HEAVENLY PLACES

"But God, who is rich in mercy, for his great love wherewith he loved us, ⁵ Even when we were dead in sins, hath quickened us together with Christ, (by grace ye are saved;)⁶ And hath raised us up together, and made us sit together in heavenly places in Christ Jesus" (Ephesians 2:4-6; KJV).

This is our true spiritual position, and we need to approach this life from this viewpoint. When we pray, we must pray from this spiritual reality. The scriptures also tell us that we have been made priests and kings unto God (Revelation 1:6).

Raised together with Christ is a position of authority in Christ. We are actually sitting together in heavenly places in Christ. Could this be why the evil spirit that the sons of Sceva were trying to cast out said to them: *"Jesus I know, and Paul I know; but who are ye?"* (Act 19:15). They were not in Christ; therefore, they had no authority.

What a privilege it is to be in Christ!

Prayer: Father, I thank You for raising me up together with Christ and sitting me together in heavenly places in Christ. By your grace, I will use this privilege to bring glory to your name in Jesus' name.

Day 7: Blessed with all Spiritual Blessings

Blessed be the God and Father of our Lord Jesus Christ, who has blessed us with every spiritual blessing in the heavenly places in Christ (Ephesians 1:3).

This scripture tells us that we are blessed, not some, but with all spiritual blessings in heavenly places in Christ.

As we are in Christ, we partake of what Christ has. Jesus Christ is seated in heavenly places, and so are we (Ephesians 2:6). At that place, there are privileges, and one of them is spiritual blessings.

Prayer: Father, I thank You because You have raised me up with Christ in heavenly places. I am blessed with all spiritual blessings there. Father, I ask that You give me the revelation of what I have in You in Jesus' name. Amen.

Day 8: Chosen in Him Before the Foundation of the World

Just as He chose us in Him before the foundation of the world, that we should be holy and without blame before Him in love (Ephesians 1:4).

Just think about that. Before the foundation of the world, God chose us in Christ. That means God already saw us in Christ. The Bible also tells us that Jesus was slain from the foundation of the world (Revelation 13:8).

It is amazing that we worry about petty things, whereas we have a God who has plans for us even before the foundation of the world—billions of years ago. In light of this, we need to learn how to cast our cares upon the Lord, for nothing takes our Father by surprise.

Prayer: Father, I thank You for choosing me in Christ before the foundation of the world. This shows how much I mean to You. Thank You, Father, in Jesus' name.

Day 9: Accepted in the Beloved

To the praise of the glory of His grace, by which He [a] made us accepted in the Beloved (Ephesians 1:6).

We are now accepted in Jesus Christ. We have not been accepted by our own merit but by Jesus Christ.

This has nothing to do with our natural feelings, which can fluctuate. We are now in the Spirit (Romans 8:9), and Scripture tells us that we are accepted.

Has anyone recently rejected you? Let this truth become a higher reality than that lie, for we have been accepted in Jesus Christ.

Prayer: Father, I thank You that I have been accepted in the beloved.

Day 10: Redemption Through His Blood

In Him we have redemption through His blood, the forgiveness of sins, according to the riches of His grace (Ephesians 1:7).

We have redemption through the blood of Jesus and forgiveness of sins. What have we been redeemed from? From the curse of the law (Galatians 3:13).

We have been bought by the blood of Jesus Christ (1 Corinthians 6:20) and redeemed to God.

And they sang a new song, saying:

"You are worthy to take the scroll, And to open its seals; For You were slain, And have redeemed us to God by Your blood Out of every tribe and tongue and people and nation, And have made [d]us

kings[e] and priests to our God;And [f] we shall reign on the earth" (Revelation 5:9-10).

What a treasure we have in Christ! We are now the people of God because of the blood of Jesus Christ.

Prayer: Father, I thank You for redeeming me by the blood of Jesus Christ. Thank You, Jesus, for shedding Your blood for me.

Day 11: We Have Obtained an Inheritance

In Him also we have obtained an inheritance, being predestined according to the purpose of Him who works all things according to the counsel of His will (Ephesians 1:11).

In the natural, we don't need to do anything to obtain an inheritance. Automatically, an inheritance belongs to the person whose name it is in. All the person has to do is claim it.

This scripture tells us that we have obtained an inheritance in Christ. It also says that we are heirs of God and joint heirs with Christ (Romans 8:17). The Holy Spirit is the foretaste of our inheritance in Christ.

The Spirit is the [e]guarantee [the first instalment, the pledge, a foretaste] of our inheritance until the redemption of God's own [purchased] possession [His believers], to the praise of His glory (Ephesians 1:14; AMP).

Blessed be the God and Father of our Lord Jesus Christ, who according to His abundant mercy has begotten us again to a living hope through the resurrection of Jesus Christ from the dead, ⁴ to an inheritance [b] incorruptible and undefiled and that does not fade away, reserved in heaven for you (1 Peter 1:3-4).

We have no idea what that looks like, but this is how much the Lord loves us. If you were told that the richest man in the world left an inheritance for you, your imagination would begin to paint so many wonderful things.

We have obtained an inheritance in Christ.

Prayer: Father, I thank You for the inheritance that I have obtained in Christ. Lord, I ask for spiritual understanding and a revelation of what this looks like in Jesus' name.

Day 12: We are His Workmanship Created in Christ Jesus

"For we are His workmanship, created in Christ Jesus for good works, which God prepared beforehand that we should walk in them" (Ephesians 2:10).

The Lord has good works that He has prepared and ordained for us to walk in. Everyone in Christ is a partaker of the heavenly calling (Hebrews 3:1).

Isn't it a privilege to be God's workmanship? The Lord has great plans for each and every one of us to fulfil. As we pursue the Lord and seek the kingdom of God, His plans will be revealed to us.

Prayer: Father, I thank You that I am created in Christ Jesus for good works. Father, I say yes to the great plans You have for me in Your kingdom, in Jesus' name. Amen.

Day 13: Near to God by the Blood of Jesus

But now [at this very moment] in Christ Jesus you who once were [so very] far away [from God] have been brought near [b]by the blood of Christ (Ephesians 2:13; AMP).

Now that we are in Christ, the blood of Jesus Christ has brought us near to God. We need to meditate on this and be renewed in the spirit of our minds that we are now near to God because of the blood of Jesus Christ, our Lord. Have you ever seen someone with such a close walk with the Father that you desired the same? The good news is, this is available to every believer in Christ. We just need to learn how to cultivate our fellowship with the Lord.

Prayer: Father, I thank You for the blood of Jesus, which has brought me near unto You. I now have access because of the sacrifice of Jesus—His blood that He shed for me. Thank You, Lord.

Day 14: We Access to the Father

And He came and preached peace to you who were afar off and to those who were near for through Him we both have access by one Spirit to the Father (Ephesians 2:17-18).

Did you know that we all have access by one Spirit to the Father? Have you ever run from pillar to post looking for someone to pray for you? While others praying for us is necessary sometimes, the good news is that we all have the same access to the Father by one Spirit.

Jesus Christ has paved the way for us. Have you desired a close walk with the Lord that you observed in someone else? The good news is that this is available to us all. We just have to pay the price. There is no respect of persons with God (Romans

2:11). While some sit in front of the TV, others spend time in the presence of the Lord. We all have the same access; we just need to prioritise our time with the Lord's help and grace.

Prayer: Father, I thank You for now having access to You because of the price Jesus Christ, my Lord and Saviour, paid.

Day 15: All the Promises of God Are Yes in Christ

For all the promises of God in Him are Yes, and in Him Amen, to the glory of God through us (2 Corinthians 1:20).

When we claim and declare God's promises, the answer is yes because of Jesus Christ. The promises of God are to be manifested through us to the glory of God.

"For all of God's promises have been fulfilled in Christ with a resounding "Yes!" And through Christ, our "Amen" (which means "Yes") ascends to God for his glory" (2 Corinthians 1:20; NLT).

So, when we pray or declare God's truth, it is not about us. It is all about Jesus Christ. Our confidence is in what Jesus Christ has accomplished for us. With this reality, doubt will have no place in us because we know it is all about Jesus. This should be our perspective when we approach the promises of God. We just need to meditate on the price that Jesus Christ paid for us.

Prayer: Father, I thank You that all your promises are yes and amen. You hear me, and I can claim Your promises because of Jesus Christ.

Day 16: The Righteousness of God in Him

For He made Him who knew no sin to be sin for us, that we might become the righteousness of God in Him (2 Corinthians 5:21).

Jesus Christ became sin for us so that we could become God's righteousness in Christ. We now have right standing with God because of what Jesus Christ did for us. Our righteousness is all because of Jesus, and this is not of ourselves.

In the Book of Romans, we can see more about our righteousness in Christ.

"21 But now the righteousness of God apart from the law is revealed, being witnessed by the Law and the Prophets, 22 even the righteousness of God, through faith in Jesus Christ, to all [f] and on

all who believe. For there is no difference, ^{23} for all have sinned and fall short of the glory of God, ^{2}" (Romans 3:21-23).

Have you seen anyone so bold in their faith that you desired a similar boldness? According to scripture, there is no difference. Everyone in Christ has the same right standing with God. The reason one person expresses this more in their walk in faith than another is simply awareness and revelation. There is no difference. We have all been made righteousness in Christ.

Prayer: Father, I thank You that I am now the righteousness of God in Christ. Thank You, Father, that I now have right standing with You.

Day 17: God Dwells in Us

Whoever confesses that Jesus is the Son of God, God abides in him, and he in God (1 John 4:15).

The scriptures tell us that God now lives in us, and we in God. God lives in us. Further, this scripture says that our bodies are now the temple of the Holy Spirit (1 Corinthians 6:19), and our body and spirit belong to God (1 Corinthians 6:20). What a privilege and honour!

We need to meditate on the fact that God now lives in us, and we are in God. Hence, walking in the revelation of this reality will bring a greater dimension to our Christian walk.

Prayer: Father, thank You that You now live in me and I in You. I ask for grace to have a revelation of this so that I can begin to walk in the consciousness of it in Jesus' name. Amen.

DAY 18: WE ARE IN CHRIST

*And we know that the Son of God has come and has given us an understanding, that we may know Him who is true; and **we are in Him who is true, in His Son Jesus Christ**. This is the true God and eternal life* (1 John 5:20).

The scripture tells us that we are in Jesus Christ, and this is part of what eternal life is all about. We need to picture and image ourselves in Christ, for this is where we really are. As we walk in the revelation of this spiritual reality, we will walk in great authority. We must remember that all authority in heaven and on earth has been given to Jesus Christ, our Lord (Matthew 28:18). We have been told to go in the name of the Lord, and as we go, we must visualise ourselves going in Him and His name. This is because we are in Christ.

IN CHRIST

Next time we are in a position to exercise our authority, we should do it gladly, knowing that we are in Christ.

Prayer: Father, I thank You that I am now in Christ. This is eternal life, being in Christ. I ask for revelation knowledge to begin to walk in the reality of this truth in Jesus' name. Amen.

Day 19: We Are Saved From Wrath Through Him

Much more then, having now been justified by His blood, we shall be saved from wrath through Him (Romans 5:9).

We have been saved from the wrath to come through Jesus Christ.

"And to wait for his Son from heaven, whom he raised from the dead, even Jesus, which delivered us from the wrath to come" (1 Thessalonians 1:10).

Jesus Christ has delivered us from the wrath to come. Next time you hear about the wrath to come, there should be no concern for those in Christ. This is one reason we need to preach the gospel to those that do not know the Lord. There is a wrath to come, and the only way to be delivered from it is by accepting the sacrifice that Jesus paid for us.

We also need to remind those who have grown cold for whatever reason that the truth is they cannot afford to. Too much is at stake. We must not allow the enemy to steal the treasure that we have in Christ. The spiritual realm is real, disguised by present comfort and distractions, which will all fade away.

"While we do not look at the things which are seen, but at the things which are not seen. For the things which are seen are temporary, but the things which are not seen are eternal" (2 Corinthians 4:18).

Prayer: Father, l thank You for delivering me from the wrath to come. Thank You, Jesus, for paying the ultimate price by becoming a man and laying down Your life for me.

Day 20: More Than Conquerors Through Him

Who shall separate us from the love of Christ? Shall tribulation, or distress, or persecution, or famine, or nakedness, or peril, or sword? 36 As it is written:

"For Your sake we are killed all day long; We are accounted as sheep for the slaughter."

37 Yet in all these things we are more than conquerors through Him who loved us (Romans 8:35–37).

We are in this world, but we do not belong to this world (John 17:16). We will have trials, persecutions, and difficult times, but the scriptures tell us that we are not just conquerors but more than conquerors through Him who loved us.

In other words, our victory is through the One that loved us. That is a victory ground shout. Do you have something boasting against you? Tell it that you are more than a conqueror through Christ Jesus, our Lord.

Prayer: Father, I thank You for Your love for me and for showing me that I am more than a conqueror through Jesus Christ, my Lord.

Day 21: Enriched By Him

I thank my God always concerning you for the grace of God which was given to you by Christ Jesus, ⁵ that you were enriched in everything by Him in all [b]utterance and all knowledge (1 Corinthians 1:4-5).

Our Lord and Saviour, Jesus Christ, enriches us in all utterances and knowledge. In other words, knowing Jesus Christ brings supernatural enrichment into our lives.

Have you been tasked to share the gospel or flow in whatever gift the Lord has given you? You can ask for the Lord to give you an utterance. Do you need knowledge in an area? You can ask for knowledge. We need to acknowledge that the source of our utterance and knowledge is Jesus Christ.

IN CHRIST

Prayer: Father, I thank You, for I am enriched in all utterance and knowledge through Jesus Christ, my Lord and Saviour.

Day 22: We live through Him

In this the love of God was manifested toward us, that God has sent His only begotten Son into the world, that we might live through Him (1 John 4:9).

This scripture confirms why God sent Jesus Christ to die for us so that we might live through Him. Isn't it great that we do not need to live in this life in our own strength? We are empowered by Him.

Another scripture that highlights our great privilege in Christ can be found in the Book of Galatians.

"I have been crucified with Christ; it is no longer I who live, but Christ lives in me; and the life which I now live in the flesh I live

by faith in the Son of God, who loved me and gave Himself for me" (Galatians 2:20).

This scripture tells us that the life that we now live in the flesh is lived by faith in the Son of God. It is talking about our physical walk in this world.

Prayer: Father, thank You for sending Jesus to die for me so that l might live through Him. Therefore, l walk in wisdom and victory in this life because l live through Christ.

Day 23: Called unto the Fellowship of His Son

God is faithful, by whom you were called into the fellowship of His Son, Jesus Christ our Lord (1 Corinthians 1:9).

We are called unto the fellowship of Jesus Christ, our Lord. Have you found anyone that you admire for how they walk with the Lord? We all have access to walk in fellowship with the Lord. What is fellowship? Fellowship is mutual communication, the sharing of mutual interests. This is what we have been called into.

God is faithful, by whom you were called into the fellowship of his Son, Jesus Christ our Lord (ESV).

IN CHRIST

Prayer: Father, I thank You, and You have called me into the fellowship of your Son, Jesus Christ. Lord, I ask for spiritual understanding on how to walk in the reality of this in Jesus' name. Amen.

Day 24: We are Now Light in the Lord

For you were once darkness, but now you are light in the Lord. Walk as children of light (Ephesians 5:8).

Jesus is the light of the world (John 8:12). In Him was life, and the life was the light of men (John 1:4). As we are in Christ, we are in the light. This is what the scripture says in the Book of Ephesians. We are now light in the Lord.

I have heard some Christians testify that people have walked up to them and told them they saw light. This is simply who we are now in the spirit. We are light in the Lord. Wherever we go, we can shine the light of Jesus to others.

IN CHRIST

Prayer: Father, thank You, as I am now light in the Lord. I will walk in the power of this light in Jesus' Name. Amen.

Day 25: We Are Now Sons of God

"But as many as received him, to them gave he power to become the sons of God, even to them that believe on his name" (John 1:12).

We are now sons of God. The scripture also tells us that we have been adopted as children of God.

"For you did not receive the spirit of bondage again to fear, but you received the Spirit of adoption by whom we cry out, 'Abba,[e] Father.' 16 The Spirit Himself bears witness with our spirit that we are children of God" (Romans 8:15-16).

The Holy Spirit bears witness with our spirits that we are now the children of God. This is what Jesus Christ has made available to us.

IN CHRIST

Prayer: Father, I thank You that I am now Your child.

Day 26: Joint Heirs with Christ

The Spirit Himself bears witness with our spirit that we are children of God, ^{17} and if children, then heirs—heirs of God and joint heirs with Christ, if indeed we suffer with Him, that we may also be glorified together (Romans 8:16-17).

The scriptures tell us that we are the heirs of God. Because of God, our Father, and the Father of our Lord Jesus Christ, we are joint heirs with Christ because we share the same Father.

This spiritual reality needs to dawn on us. Let us meditate on it and begin to live in its practical application. We must see ourselves the way God the Father sees us—joint heirs with Christ. We must not allow the world to mould us, nor should we permit negative circumstances of life to dictate who we are.

IN CHRIST

We are heirs of God, the One who made heaven and earth—the Ancient of Days, and joint heirs with Christ.

Prayer: Father, I thank You for making me an heir, and I am a joint heir with Christ.

Day 27: Our Old Man Is Crucified with Him

Knowing this, that our old man is crucified with him, that the body of sin might be destroyed, that henceforth we should not serve sin (Romans 6:6; KJV).

When Jesus Christ was crucified, our old man was crucified with Him. Another scripture puts it this way:

"Who his own self bare our sins in his own body on the tree, that we, being dead to sins, should live unto righteousness: by whose stripes ye were healed" (1 Peter 2:24).

We are no longer slaves to sin because our old man was crucified with Christ on the cross. In Christ, we have victory over sin. This is a supernatural advantage that we have in Christ.

IN CHRIST

"Let not sin therefore reign in your mortal body, that ye should obey it in the lusts thereof. ¹³ Neither yield ye your members as instruments of unrighteousness unto sin: but yield yourselves unto God, as those that are alive from the dead, and your members as instruments of righteousness unto God. ¹⁴ For sin shall not have dominion over you: for ye are not under the law, but under grace" (Romans 6:12-14).

Prayer: Father, I thank You that I can now yield my members as instruments of righteousness because of what Christ has done for me.

Day 28: We Are to Walk as He Walked

He who says he abides in Him ought himself also to walk just as He walked (1 John 2:6).

The scriptures tell us that we now abide in Christ. *Whosoever abideth in him sinneth not: whosoever sinneth hath not seen him, neither known him* (1 John 3:6; KJV).

"Hereby know we that we dwell in him, and he in us, because he hath given us of his Spirit" (1 John 4:13).

The above scriptures show that we dwell in Him and He dwells in us. 1 John 2 tells us that we are responsible for walking as He walked. That is our yardstick.

Day 29: We Have Eternal Life

And we know that the Son of God is come, and hath given us an understanding, that we may know him that is true, and we are in him that is true, even in his Son Jesus Christ. This is the true God, and eternal life (1 John 5:20).

Jesus Christ has come, and He has given us an understanding. The scripture further tells us we are in Him, and this is the true God and eternal life.

Eternal life is knowing Jesus Christ and the true God.

The Book of John also defines eternal life:

"And this is life eternal, that they might know thee the only true God, and Jesus Christ, whom thou hast sent" (John 17:3).

Our being in Christ gives us access to eternal life.

For the wages of sin is death; but the gift of God is eternal life through Jesus Christ our Lord (Romans 6:23).

(*For the life was manifested, and we have seen it, and bear witness, and shew unto you that eternal life, which was with the Father, and was manifested unto us*;) (1 John 2:1).

Prayer: Father, I thank You that I have eternal life because I am now in Christ.

Day 30: No Condemnation to Those in Christ Jesus

There is therefore now no condemnation to those who are in Christ Jesus, who[a] do not walk according to the flesh, but according to the Spirit (Romans 8:1).

The qualifying phrase in this verse is *"those that do not walk after the flesh but after the spirit"*. And this applies to those in Christ Jesus.

There will be times when the Lord will instruct us to do things that others around us may not necessarily understand. It might even look contrary to popular opinion, and others might want to say things that do not align with God's plan. The Lord says there is no condemnation to those in Him who walk after the Spirit.

Another vital lesson in this verse is that when we see ourselves the way God sees us, we will walk according to God's word and perspective: there is no condemnation. For example, repent and ask the Lord to forgive you if you do something wrong. The Lord forgives, and we should forgive ourselves and move on. The world may say something different, but there is no condemnation to those in Christ Jesus who do not walk after the flesh but after the Spirit. We win in Him when we stay in the Spirit.

Prayer: Father, I thank you that there is no condemnation to those in Christ Jesus who walk not after the flesh but after the Spirit. I am grateful!

Day 31: Greater Is He That Is in You

*Hereby know ye the Spirit of God: Every spirit that confesseth that Jesus Christ is come in the flesh is of God: ³ And every spirit that confesseth not that Jesus Christ is come in the flesh is not of God: and this is that spirit of antichrist, whereof ye have heard that it should come; and even now already is it in the world. ⁴ Ye are of God, little children, and have overcome them: because **greater is he that is in you, than he that is in the world*** (1 John 4:2-4).

Looking at the last verse in its proper setting, this scripture reminds us that we are of God, and greater is He who is in us than he who is in the world. Why is this scripture telling us this? It is because of what is around us. The Bible calls it "the spirit of antichrist."

So, next time someone says something contrary to the truth and is yielding to a spirit not of God, be reminded that greater is He that is in you.

Prayer: Father, I thank you that greater is He that is in me. Christ lives in me.

Day 32: We Always Triumph in Christ

Now thanks be unto God, which always causeth us to triumph in Christ, and maketh manifest the savour of his knowledge by us in every place. For we are unto God a sweet savour of Christ, in them that are saved, and in them that perish (2 Corinthians 2:14; KJV).

"Now thanks be to God who always leads us in triumph in Christ, and through us [d]diffuses the fragrance of His knowledge in every place. 15 For we are to God the fragrance of Christ among those who are being saved and among those who are perishing" (2 Corinthians 2:14-15)

In Christ Jesus, we always triumph. In other words, we win. Now notice the word "triumph". The American dictionary defines "triumph" as follows: *"A complete victory or success achieved especially after great difficulties making the result particularly satisfactory"*.

Are you going through a difficult time? Are you in Christ? Then, know that in Christ, we always triumph. The Lord fights our battles, and as we engage Him by praying and doing whatever we are led to do, we triumph. Triumphing in Christ is a promise for us. We need to meditate on this scripture, especially during difficult times and seasons.

Not only do we triumph in Christ, but this scripture tells us that we diffuse the fragrance of His knowledge in every place. Therefore, people see the goodness of God in our lives.

Don't allow the enemy to lie to you. You might be going through a rough patch now, but God always causes us to triumph in Christ.

Prayer: Father, I thank You for always causing me to triumph in Christ. I am grateful for this victory in whatever I might face in Jesus' name.

Day 33: : In Christ, the Veil Is Taken Away From Our Hearts

1 *³ And not as Moses, which put a veil over his face, that the children of Israel could not stedfastly look to the end of that which is abolished: ¹⁴ But their minds were blinded: for until this day remaineth the same vail untaken away in the reading of the old testament; which vail is done away in Christ. ¹⁵ But even unto this day, when Moses is read, the vail is upon their heart. ¹⁶ Nevertheless when it shall turn to the Lord, the vail shall be taken away* (2 Corinthians 3:14-16; KJV).

"*But their minds were blinded. For until this day the same veil remains unlifted in the reading of the Old Testament, because the veil is taken away in Christ. ¹⁵ But even to this day, when Moses is read, a veil lies on their heart. ⁱ⁶ Nevertheless when one turns to the Lord, the veil is taken away* (2 Corinthians 3:14-16).

Have you ever heard someone say they don't understand the Bible when reading it? It takes the Lord through the person of the Holy Spirit to give us an understanding of the scriptures. This veil symbolises that the block to access understanding and revelation knowledge is done away with in Christ. When our hearts turn to the Lord, the veil is taken away.

Every understanding and revelation we receive from Scripture is because the Lord has opened our hearts.

Prayer: Thank You, Lord, for opening up my heart to truth and revelation. This is a privilege that I have in Christ, and I am grateful for it in Jesus' name.

Day 34: We Are All One in Christ

There is neither Jew nor Greek, there is neither slave nor free, there is neither male nor female; for you are all one in Christ Jesus (Galatians 3:28).

Have you ever been to a foreign land and encountered believers in Christ for the first time? Isn't it amazing that we can all see things the same way?

This is simply because, in Christ, we are all one. The Scripture describes it this way: *"In whom the whole family in heaven and earth is named"* (Ephesians 3:15).

The Bible tells us that there is neither slave nor free, male nor female, Jew or Greek. In Christ, we are all one.

We need to discern and see ourselves this way.

Prayer: Father, I thank You for making me part of a larger family because of what Jesus has done for me.

DAY 35: DEAD UNTO SIN AND ALIVE UNTO GOD

Likewise you also, [c]reckon yourselves to be dead indeed to sin, but alive to God in Christ Jesus our Lord (Romans 6:11).

Another scripture puts it this way: *"Who his own self bare our sins in his own body on the tree, that we, being dead to sins, should live unto righteousness: by whose stripes ye were healed"* (1 Peter 2:24).

Because of what Jesus Christ did for us, we are now dead to sin. The scriptures tell us that *"sin shall no longer have dominion over us"* (Romans 6:14). This is a benefit we now have in Christ.

We have also been made alive unto God. We can fellowship with God because we are now in Christ.

We need to remind ourselves that we are now alive unto God.

Prayer: Father, I thank You for being alive unto You in Christ.

Day 36: God Loves Us as He Loves Jesus

I in them, and You in Me; that they may be made perfect in one, and that the world may know that You have sent Me, and have loved them as You have loved Me (John 17:23).

From this scripture, we can again see that Christ is in us. He lives in us. Not only that, but this scripture tells us that God loves us as He loves Jesus. That is simply amazing! Indeed, we do need a revelation of the love of God. This will greatly impact our fellowship with the Father and our walk in this life.

This shows that we have so many privileges in Christ.

Prayer: Thank you, Father, for loving me as you love Jesus. I ask for a deeper revelation of this in Jesus' name. Amen.

Day 37: We Have Put on Christ

For as many of you as were baptized into Christ have put on Christ (Galatians 3:27).

We are now baptised into Christ; hence, we have put on Christ. What does this look like? Again, this is something we need to meditate on. In the natural, when we put something on, it protects us, and we represent what we put on. In other words, the flavour of what we put on is now our identity. In a nutshell, we have put on Christ.

This should also be reflected in the way we conduct ourselves. We must now remember that we have put on Christ.

Prayer: Father, l thank You for baptising me into Christ; therefore, l have put on Christ. Father, l ask for a revelation of this in Jesus' name.

DAY 38: WE HAVE THE PROMISE OF THE HOLY SPIRIT

Christ has redeemed us from the curse of the law, having become a curse for us (for it is written, "Cursed is everyone who hangs on a tree"), that the blessing of Abraham might come upon the Gentiles in Christ Jesus, that we might receive the promise of the Spirit through faith" (Galatians 3:13-14).

In Christ Jesus, we are promised the Holy Spirit. The Holy Spirit is a gift for every believer in Christ.

"Then Peter said to them, "Repent, and let every one of you be baptized in the name of Jesus Christ for the [k]remission of sins; and you shall receive the gift of the Holy Spirit. 39 For the promise is to you and to your children, and to all who are afar off, as many as the Lord our God will call (Acts 2:38-39).

The Holy Spirit is a person who has come to stay and abide with us (John 14:16). The Holy Spirit has many roles in the lives of believers in Christ. Have you received Him yet?

Prayer: Father, I thank You for the Holy Spirit. I ask for grace to develop my walk with the Holy Spirit, who has come to help me in this life.

Day 39: In Christ, Our Faith Works Through Love

For in Jesus Christ neither circumcision availeth any thing, nor uncircumcision; but faith which worketh by love (Galatians 5:6; KJV).

For in Christ Jesus neither circumcision nor uncircumcision avails anything, but faith working through love (Galatians 5:6).

Now that we are in Christ, we walk by faith and not by sight (2 Corinthians 5:7). Scripture tells us that our faith works by love.

When we have a revelation of how much the Lord loves us and we know that God is love (1 John 4:16), this will boost our faith. This is a perspective that we need to have in our faith.

God is love, and He loves us. Therefore, we know that God is on our side.

Prayer: Father l thank you my faith works through love. Father l ask for a greater revelation of your love for me in Jesus Name. Amen.

Day 40: In Him We Have Peace

These things I have spoken to you, that in Me you may have peace. In the world you [f]will have tribulation; but be of good cheer, I have overcome the world (John 16:33).

Jesus told us that He gives us His peace (John 14:27). In the scripture quoted above, the Lord says that we have peace in Him. The Lord further tells us that in the world we will have tribulation.

We need to learn to live in the peace of our Lord and Saviour, Jesus Christ. There might be trouble and challenges around us, but we can keep ourselves in the peace of God. This is a privilege for those in Christ.

How do we keep ourselves in the peace of the Lord that is already available to us in Christ?

First, it is by staying our minds on the Lord:

You will keep him in perfect peace, Whose mind is stayed on You, Because he trusts in You (Isaiah 26:3).

Second, it is also by taking everything to the Lord in prayer

⁶ Be anxious for nothing, but in everything by prayer and supplication, with thanksgiving, let your requests be made known to God; ⁷ and the peace of God, which surpasses all understanding, will guard your hearts and minds through Christ Jesus (Philippians 4:6-7).

When we take everything to the Lord in prayer, the peace of God will keep guarding our hearts and minds through Christ Jesus.

God is a God of peace (Hebrews 13:20).

We need to learn to yield and keep ourselves in the peace available to us in Christ Jesus.

Prayer: Father, I thank You for the peace I have in Christ. Thank you for the grace to keep me in your peace at all times, in Jesus' name. Amen.

SALVATION PRAYER

Father God, I come to you in Jesus' name. I admit that I am a sinner, and I now receive the sacrifice that Jesus Christ paid for me.

I confess with my mouth the Lord Jesus, and I believe in my heart that God raised Him from the dead.

I now declare that Jesus Christ is my Lord and Saviour.

Thank you, Father, for saving me in Jesus' name.

I am now your child. Amen.

If you've said this prayer for the first time, send an email to Bisiwriter@gmail.com . Start reading your Bible and ask the Lord to guide you to a good church.

BISI OLADIPUPO

ABOUT THE AUTHOR

Bisi Oladipupo has been a Christian for many years and lives in the United Kingdom with her family.

Her academic journey is a testament to her commitment to understanding and sharing the Word of God. She has attended prestigious Bible colleges, earned a diploma in Biblical Studies from a UK Bible college, and obtained a Bachelor's degree in Bible and Theology from a renowned USA School of Ministry.

She teaches God's Word and coordinates Bible studies and a Christian fellowship.

Her website is www.bisiwrites.com

You can contact Bisi by email at bisiwriter@gmail.com

Also by

1. The Twelve Apostles of Jesus Christ: Lessons We Can Learn

2. The Lord's Cup in Communion: The Significance of taking the Lord's Supper

3. Different Ways to Receive Healing from Scripture and Walk in Health

4. Believing on The Name of Jesus Christ: What Every Believer Needs to Know

5. The Mind and Your Christian Walk: The Impact of the mind on our Christian walk

6. Relationship Skills in the Bible: Scriptural Principles of relating to others

IN CHRIST

7. The Nature of God's Kingdom: The Characteristics of the Kingdom of God

8. The Person of the Holy Spirit

9. 41 Insights from the Book of Revelation

10. The Importance of Spiritual Discernment

11. God Speaks Through Nature

12. It's All About the Heart

13. A Better Covenant: A Look at the Covenants of God and Our Better Covenant

14. 40 Day New Covenant Devotional

15. What Happens When We Pray?

16. Daily Bread for Healing: A 40-day Healing Devotional

17. 40 Facts of Who Jesus Is: A Devotional

18. 50 Prayers for Your Children and Generations to Come

19. The Grace of God: Why We Need It

20. The Importance of Spiritual Understanding

BISI OLADIPUPO

www.ingramcontent.com/pod-product-compliance
Lightning Source LLC
Chambersburg PA
CBHW030043100526
44590CB00011B/310